exhort the goddesses

ALSO BY ERIKA ATKINSON

*Happily Lost in Time and Place*

*Frozen Stillness: A Journey to Antarctica*

*More Miles and Moments: Still Happily Lost*

# exhort
## THE goddesses

erika atkinson

AGELOFF
BOOKS

ISBN-13: 978-0692471500 (Ageloff Books)
ISBN-10: 0692471502

For additional information about Erika Atkinson,
you may contact her by email at erikainparis@sbcglobal.net.

*Design by Randall Friesen*

Printed in the United States of America.

*In the spirit of Gilles Jéronymos*

*and*

*For Bruno Bieth*

# CONTENTS

## III. WONDER AND WORTHINESS

## IV.  ALL OVER THE PLANET

## acknowledgments

Oversized thanks, endless gratitude, and so much love to Randall Friesen at Ageloff Press, New York, for formatting my work with expertise, creativity, enthusiasm, and brilliance.

As always, heartfelt gratitude to Sean Owens for his invaluable and intelligent counsel, particularly his insightful suggestions in this big adventure.

Many sincere thanks to Dean Kostos for the kindness of believing in me and bringing this opportunity to a reality for me.

And love to Michael Welch for being there, at all times and in all ways.

You will hear thunder and remember me,
and think:
she wanted storms . . .

—*Anna Akhmatova*

# I.

# elegies to the moon

# BLUE AUGUST MOON

large
full
round
blue
luminous
radiant

the second moon of this month

dangling from the clearest indigo sky
leaning into my window like a prostitute
delicious enough to take a bite

la luna super has no prejudice
she is the romance of the cosmic universe
she glows down upon earthlings shedding equal light on all
she proportions her unobscured luster equally for everyone

i'm sipping a perfect bordeaux
my back to the bar audience
my wine glass empty
i kiss its rim
with cold lips
and disappear home
her moonship guiding me along

she wonders about me
i wonder about her
she probably has answers
i have none

don't want answers . . .

# BENT AND SILVER

noble crescent moon

there it hangs
top of sixteenth street
balanced like a seesaw
waiting
    waiting for a smile
        waiting in cold silence
            waiting for acknowledgement

there it hangs
omnipresent
between tall buildings
    a strong hyphen
between concrete walls
    a shining beam
at the end of the street
    a watch guard
in my back yard
    a greeting through my window

# A SPECIAL MOON

a crisp icy moon
shining with distinguished brilliance
into this brisk january night
i speed-walk while sporadic clouds cover her
creating playful shadows

looking up is a connection
from me to you
    via the moon

please find a moment to gaze at her
    with awe

she is the symbol of the heartbeat

# THE IN BETWEEN

The In Between
In Life
In Practice
Always A Little Missing
Or Never Enough There
The Unfair Turbulence
The Unjust Equity
Wanting To Be Righted
Perhaps One Day
Under The Super Moon
Twelve Percent Closer On The Apogee
What Is The Other 'gee'?
It Doesn't Matter

The Other 'gee' Is Perigee

# NOT MY FAVORITE

old lady gibbous up there
hanging glibly in the sky
not my favorite

but she is up there
bloated to half
watching
glaring
as i pass by
not my favorite

still
i challenge her
but she rules the sky
not my favorite

i challenge her
because i feel stronger than she is
not my favorite

*II.*

# heart nuggets

# FRAGILE INTERLUDE

i think . . .

. . . sometimes

life is too short

the truly beautiful things
are often too far apart

yet
the shortness of life
is lengthened
when a moment of affinity
    a sensitivity
       an understanding
          is shared
             is realized

i call this moment a fragile interlude

# GRATITUDE

awakening early this morning
a wave of gratitude drifts over me
sliding my hands across my warm breasts
i feel secretly ambushed by the sensation of their softness
immediately gratified that they are there
for a private tactile moment

my fortune is rare and good
of that i am easily persuaded

# AT LOVE

*[for Michael]*

naked
he knew my thoughts
gold jewelry displayed around my neck
a sage green scarf adorning my shoulders
and confident
astride his lap

i felt the hips of a god
joined with mine

the earth shuddered a flamboyant sigh

# AUTUMN VELVET COUCH

ten pm
on an autumn velvet couch
    stretched the length of a pacific heights room
two parallel bodies
floating through all seas of sensibility
old ruminations
obliterated by new consonant kissing dialogue
desirous minutes passing by
and passing by

this voyage
i am the land-bound stone
that has received its awakening
its re-inclusion
as it drifts away from a gray indifferent shore

inspired nows turning into always moments

here in the foggy stillness of a lusty night
i charge you
with reinvention of me

# TWO PARALLEL BEINGS

two parallel beings
content in solemn nocturnal peace

then
    alas
        it is dawn

morning pronounces itself

a cataclysmal mix of selfless and selfish

# SURRENDERED

i surrendered
to one look from you

now i am gathering the sky and the planets
in hopeful exchange
for one kiss from you

# THE SHORTEST DISTANCE

a kiss
   a singular bond
   a naked promise
   an eloquent confection
   an electric touch
   a rousing resonance
   a crystallized moment
   an ephemeral adventure
   a final surrender
   an instant change
   a lingering memory

a kiss
   the shortest distance between you and me

# THE GIFT OF LONELINESS

it added beauty to my days
    when none seemed imminent
it put a special burn on sunsets
    when a paintbrush wasn't in sight
it turned the trees into ethereal silhouettes
    when the wind had calmed at evening
it made the night-time air smell better
    when fry-shops had closed
it made my midnight gait seem lighter
    when i sensed you soundly sleeping somewhere
it made my smile wider
    when my lips were closed
it made my eyes look deeper
    when silence abounded around
it caused my heart to dance gently
    when my inner springs felt dried up
it indulged me in the great art of non-conversation
    when you weren't there
it helped me form resolutions
    when abandonment felt too close

it expressed glories
    with awe
it expressed pain
    with knowledge

it was the gift of loneliness

# WITH YOU

with you

not going anywhere
just being there
where is there
there is here
together with you
you with me
here
there
anywhere
everywhere

but never nowhere

with you

no special topic
no specific theme
just you
here
me
here
we
here
together here

but never not

something very much worth celebrating

## OF ME

deep within the glowing chambers of me
is a continuously glowing you
a baudelarian flower of rarest bloom
which no socratic crypticisms will ever erase

## COMPLETENESS

ready

waiting

you arrive

bolts of lightning tear through my heart
stinging tingles crawl up my spine

here
next to you
my hand caressing your thigh
as i watch a humus–slathered biscuit travel mouthward

here
in the familiar comfort of my parlor
a peaceful space
completed by you

here
where we tell one another the story we are

# FREEDOM

i have a thousand lips
pink and white and sweet as peony
they want to lick your face

somewhere under my heartcage
my breath becomes thin as the skin of dried grass

my teeth are basting kisses to your face

my legs are anchored to your height

it is a beautiful world

# III.
## wonder and worthiness

# MID-TERM ELECTION DAY: 2014

a time of separated feelings
    intensified with groans and sighs

political news announcements
    burned into my psyche
        like the sting of a leather whip

poisoning us all across the nation
    reprehensible corruption
        poverty of intelligence
            frustration and annoyance

caught in a lingering anger
    well seasoned with an expletive or two

watching a few drooping heads walk by my wine bar window
    in the autumn's almost-full moonlight
        reassures nothing

geniality of guests at the bar
    taking for granted their luxury
        their privacy
            their space
                is making me ill at ease

somewhere up there
    a thousand stars need to begin to flash hope
        across a doomed sky

I feel very alone within this inscrutable society

# CASTRO CHRISTMAS DREAMING

standing at market and castro
beneath the proud rainbow flag
looking eastward
all the way to the ferry building
bounteous red bows
hugging rows of palms
along the busy boulevard

standing at market and castro
beneath the proud rainbow flag
looking southward
one thousand strings of tiny white lights
cheering one hundred trees
along the busy avenue

along castro street

    endless merchant windows dressed
    for the passerby's wonder

    diesel men's wear
    animated fashion shoppers

    ferrari's deli
    animated cuisinists

    blush bar
    animated wine enthusiasts

walgreens
animated obama dolls

cliff's
animated cross–dressers

castro theatre
animated sing–a–longers

twin peaks tavern
animated queens

now at the corner of eighteenth and castro
standing beneath the tall and fabled christmas tree
    which is beaming
        shining
            blinking
                glowing

holiday revelers everywhere
star-filled eyes
smiles glistening
festive laughter

the entire neighborhood
holding hands
moving
no motionlessness
no stopping

and me

             sauntering

     dreaming

        observing

                feeling

      hoping

          giving

    sharing

        receiving

             participating

loving my castro life

# WINDOW GAZING

from embarcadero four on high
shifting my glance to the ferry building plaza
    a collage in constant motion
california flag
    unfurling in a limp breeze
palm fronds
    swaying to wind rhythms
        against a blue sky
fountains
    gushing effusively
    creating white watery paint strokes
        against oxidized bronze box sculptures
braceleted arms of a vintage bay bridge
    glittering variously with the sun's angles
gleaming steel gray seagulls
    flapping wings furiously
    showing no panache
        while skidding to a floppy stop on wet cobbles
colorful boutiques
    sprawled across the tiled plaza
    in all textures known to man
abstract sculptures
    here and there
    standing firm in conceptual erections
swirling cumulus clouds
    levitating over the bay waters

farm vendors
    hawking fresh green arugula
    and new red apples
vagrant dogs
    foraging for KFC leftovers
disinherited homeless outcasts
    weaving through
    their junk carts filled with detritus
        from trash canister invasions

next to my window
    lavender blossoms
        emitting fresh scent
    and bees
        buzzing
        their wings refracting light in rainbow colors

# OCTOBER JURY DUTY

jury duty
listening duty
honesty duty

the judge speaks
everyone listens
    listens fearfully

juvenile questions
authoritarian attitudes
humiliating moments

in the chambers
    bodies moving restlessly
    hearts beating anxiously
    hands shaking nervously

people wandering
    all nations
    all colors
    all equal —
        by force?
        by will?

in the justice halls
is justice served?
no one asks
no one dares
everything formulized
everything legalized

nothing warm
nothing humane
nothing natural

people of all walks
    descriptions
    countries
    professions
    creeds
    in it together
        by force?
        by will?

have you ever . . . ?
do you . . . ?
would you . . . ?
can you . . . ?

everyone —
    stalkers
    walkers
    gawkers
    talkers
        nerds
        psychiatrists
        artists
        rich bitches
        would-be engineers
        scared moms
        suburban bums

newspaper readers
slutbook readers
medical research readers
comicbook readers

gum smackers
lunch packers
computer hackers
fbi trackers
money backers

poets
historians
insurance salesmen
dancers

all in it together
by force

.

# LAND'S END

land's end
where life begins

this time
    when i get there
        i turn off to the left for a stretch
        onto a pathway unknown to me
    i find myself perched high up on a promontory
        with a view that leaves me breathless
it is early morning
the fog is rolling in
i can see the red tower tips of the golden gate bridge
i listen alone in silence
    to the roar of the sea
    to the surf pounding against the cliffside
    to the ship's plaintive horn call through the fog
barely visible
    way down below
    a very enthusiastic fisherman on a jutting rock
    doing his mightiest
    as he casts his rod out into the sea against the wind
inside me
    at this moment
        indefinable feelings
        poles of activity far apart
        horizons at both ends
        doubt and confidence
            simultaneous

i'm sitting up here
    greeting summer moths flitting by
        eager for a sunlit perch
    gaping at gulls easing their radared wings
        into foggy stillness
the fog lifts
i see naked bodies strewn amidst the rocks below
breathing
    alive
        pictoriously healthy
            camouflaged in the sand
up above
    birds
        airplanes
            jetting through the sky
                doing it easy
ahead of me
    the proudly arched golden gateway
        stretched across the last gap
            between mighty pacific waters
            and land's beginning
a fissure created by time
a feat created by man
an opportunity to enjoy it all
a city as mercurial as san francisco
    can not be captured in one moment

# SAFE ON PLANET EARTH

on a late afternoon
walking
light is slanting toward dusk
the palms along market are turning dark green
my spirit is in sweet momentum
having spent the day nowhere in particular

all dreams have been fulfilled today
neither phone nor email have dared to challenge me
from dreaming
    or completing things on my walking list

at home the radio is talking about a planet out of control
i look out my front door
    and find people traversing as always

the sun sinks completely
darkness ensues
on the boulevard stillness
    i hear palm fronds speaking to me
    about peace on the planet
if i do my part
    the web of life will continue
        so we can be in it together
            forever

# RENOIR, MOVE OVER

*[for Paola]*

renoir
move over
paola is here
it's truth on these walls
it's truth about the life we live
physical love
triangular love
just love
     as it wants to be
     as it should be
     as it is
          honest
          erotic
          sensual
          bare
in plain face of all
in naked skin for all
     mysterious
     sepia
     fuzzy
     far away
     frothing
but beckoning to my instinct
bowing to me
bending to me
bidding a welcome

# ON A SUMMER GREEN MEADOW

on a summer green meadow
the little prairie girl
aged nine
sits by a rock
pensive
alone
a few glistening butterflies for company
a few purple crocuses nearby
one is plucked to bring to her mother

here she sits
on many days
solitary
quietly dreaming of wandering
to once-upon-a-time places
imaginary for now

## IT'S ENOUGH

it's enough
    to be alive
        to see the sea
           the sky
                watch changes
                    eat
           talk
        joke
      create
    love
feel . . .

# ONE HOMELESS HEART BEATING

five o'clock in the morning
trying to get out my door to the gym
a homeless asleep on my doorstep
i step over him
hoping not to awaken him
doves in the lampshade above will guard him
i'm down the steps and across the street
to join the bodies i see through the window
cycling
my own to be momentarily included

and home again
still in the dark
up in the sky
a city moon
behind country clouds

i amble up the steps
the homeless one is gone
inside i think of him
while dripping morning coffee
i feel such gratitude
i turn and see a wooden bowl of apples and oranges
lighting up my kitchen
and wonder if he has ever seen such light

# NIGHT

they were up there tonight
in the night
high in the sky
innumerable stars
streetlights of the night

night
a world unto herself
day has eyes
but night has ears
tonight she hears me
i want to press close to her
nourish her and me

# WALKING HOME

darkness outside
creeping well beyond midnight
everything and everyone
    except me
curled up under covers
against pillows

streetmongers have gone home
homeless have crawled away
gas lamps have dimmed their glow
the night's fog is rolling down the street
    on wings of an ocean wind
shops are still and lifeless
sidewalks empty and sighing

i'm dancing on a night rainbow
singing a cloud song
before i close the shutters for the night
i exhort the goddesses
    to enter my dreams
it's warm and elevated in there

# PRIDE SUNDAY BOUQUET

tonight
walking home after the day
behind a bent man
i see a sad bouquet
off to the side
on the boulevard
white daisies
withered
silent
though still glowing in the light of the street lamp
but used
dropped
stepped on by hundreds of walking feet
i stop
i'm looking for secret meanings
but its history has ended
hopefully it was a happy ending
a few hours ago
of temporary irreplaceable rapture
and now proudly part of the debris

# SOLITUDE

solitude
    a place of stillness
    a gentle waltz in the heart

solitude
    all-encompassing
    a soul window
        that looks on everything as unity

solitude
    no need for it to be delayed until a convenient time

solitude
    in line at the supermarket
    or riding up an elevator to the thirty-ninth floor

solitude
    a presence
    not an absence
    a desire to meet silently face to face

solitude
    an experience that rewards

solitude
    the place where enthusiasm begins
        for inner adventure

solitude
    a place for connected thoughts

solitude
    where i think i will find another me . . . again

# IV.

# all over the planet

# ANTARCTICA

*[written on board ship in the Antarctic Ocean]*

hurling seas
hissing
as we bump and glide through the confluence
    toward the end of the planet

with each swell
comes a fear
a longing for one more hug

with each heave
comes a wish
a feeling that such power ought to be experienced by everyone

## FROZEN STILLNESS

*[written in Port Lockroy, Antarctica]*

Frozen whiteness
yawning to the horizon

Deep-frozen air
unendurable for human skin and eyeballs

Empty silence
reaching for the mountaintops

White mountains
soaring to twilight-painted skies

No sound
only wind wailing
ice cracking

Deep blue shadows lurking
where ice buckles and breaks

Dry valleys
screaming winds sculpting moonshapes
out of black rock

White ice
fathoms deep

Translucent blue ice
enclosed in mountainside caverns

Below white ice
darkest waters on the planet
where light has not reached in millions of years

Above white ice
a steel-gray sky
extinguishing a flaming sunset

Under white ice
water moving in giant swells
carrying earth's largest coldblooded mammals

Daylight uninterrupted
month after month

Dark sky
pierced by frozen light of a distant universe
indifferent to human existence

No roads
no cars
no houses
no people
no footsteps

And the aurora borealis dances unseen

# AMIDST SOLITARY ISLANDS

*[written on Galapagos, for JJP]*


perhaps i speak best to you
in stillness
across a wide sea
feeling like a primitive spirit
inside a displaced structure

are you listening dear friend
slowly
taking it all in

take my gratitude
    for appreciation never severed
take my love
    for gifts unselfishly given
take my thanks
    for humor unbound

i have smiles for you
    gratuitous
i promise enduring friendship
not time
    nor incident
        will take that away

# DREAM OF AN ENDED ROAD
*[written in Taipei]*


as i drove
past a grove
i arrived at a decision point in the road
and confidently turned left
    and then
    my immediate thought
    'i must survive'
all seemed ended
a cliff to the right
nothing more in sight
gravel
sand
rocks down there
a narrowing ended rock . . . to where

i was then found walking
aimlessly
upon an unblemished
newly paved road
beautifully colored blue
    with dividing yellow lines
it widened
spread into a darkness toward infinity
    i could not see where

i drifted about
    almost as though wanting to fly
    depart this earth
    but with heavy eyes
    unable to see
and everywhere
not flying
were many silver airplanes
looking like pendants

# FROM DENSE JUNGLE MISTS

*[written in Zihuatanejo]*


for some weeks
the guerrero jungle has comforted me
endorsed me with its passion

from the upper level
of a thatched roof funky beach cafe
i have watched my last sunset
    in silence
sandpipers scurrying for evening snacks
shell seekers going in for the last haul
    all colors of the sea
    all stories from the sea
    all secrets about the sea

a mist is rising above the waters
a million stars in the sky watching it
breezes beckoning from far out in the tide
every wave cresting
then crash landing
    like my breath

my last night on la ropa
the vertical surf conjoining on the shore
before retreating back to the sea
    horizontally
whispering along the strand
last words with the mermaids
neon in the moonlight

and then it's back on sixteenth street
in my neighborhood
trolleys careening along the curved track
cars honking at the big convergence
sirens screaming
bicycles whistling defiantly by
semi-trucks groaning up the long hill
people dodging traffic
dogs dodging people
cafes and bistros overflowing with cosmo addicts
nothing out of place anywhere
all as it should be

## ON PONT MARIE

*[written on Île Saint-Louis]*


i'm standing against the granite guard
of my favorite old bridge in paris
watching the sun fall into the other end of the seine
the gaslights turning on bridge by bridge
and glowing faintly
evening is descending
night is beginning
another day has gone

the sun rises
it sets
and in the time that passes
    standards are created
    values are challenged
    relationships are chosen
    obligations are dealt with
    decisions are reversed
    knowledge is acquired
    experiences are encountered
        repeated
        remembered
        sometimes forgotten

this evening
it all makes me smile
    remembering
    inside faraway mornings
    goodbyes
    down stairs
    into new days

and loveliness sets in

# THROUGH A HALF-MOON WINDOW

*[written in Paris, inspired by Jacques Prévert]*


AT MIDNIGHT

one old gas lamp, lit
    reflecting into my crooked wood-beamed room
    through ancient bubbled glass panes

assorted architectural shapes, visible
    triangles
    rectangles
    abstracts
    ovals
    formed inside four hundred years of whitewash

one narrow alley, cobbled
    glistening in the nightly mist

one tin roof, rippled
    two cats slinking to its edge
    one black
    one striped
        peering curiously at sounds below

one louvered window across the alley, open

two lovers behind it, engaged

five night revelers in the alley, strolling
    one smoking
    one laughing
    two arm in arm
    one following

one lone woman, sauntering

one amorous youth, hoping

one pair of stilettos, red
    left on the stoop
        worn down and liftless

one neon sign, orange
    wrapped around one word, *franprix*

one banner, red and black
    saying lizard lounge

three more revelers, inside
    with one tankard of ale in each left hand

one pigeon, audible
    above my window

nightfall

## AT EARLY MORNING

a ray of light, dawn

two pigeons, visible

one noisy trash truck, green

two drivers, arguing

four garbage cans, filled
    lids way up

one *supermarche* door, open

one door guard, half interested

three pigeons, very visible

## AT DAYTIME

one big *superette* window, shiny clean
    seventeen mangos, yellow-green
        in circular arrangement
    twelve apples, red
        in perfect alignment
    three *baguettes*, crisp
        in a basket

one *monsieur*, walking by

one *beret*, on *monsieur*'s head

one *madame*, in a hurried step

one pair of dolce jeans, on *madame*'s hip

one more pigeon, flying

one artist, sketching

one lovely lady, meandering

one baggy lady, attached to a leash
    pulled by a pekingese

one baby, squealing

one mother, behind it
    licking *berthillon* ice cream

several more pigeons, scurrying

## AT DUSK

one day of good things
one moment of reflective silence
one four-hundred-year-old cityscape
one more day in Paris
one grateful heart

## "POUR VOUS, LA GRANDE BLEUE!"

*[written in Collioure]*


you lap close in
you rush far out
    to sea

you hiss as you weave between jetties
you roar against salt ships
    and beyond distant sounds

you surf consistently
you are there
    always
        for ever
            and then you are gone

you are the old has–been
but remain the mysterious will–be
    was
        is
            shall–be

you churn gray with mist
you bubble up against polished sand rocks
you whisper into the cracks of concrete piers

you rise up against the horizon
    swallowing my secrets
        into your immense well

a stranger
   i came to you
      you magnetized me
         hypnotized me

a nurturer
   you welcomed me
      you covered me
         while i slept beside you a minute
         on your time-worn stone bed
      you stood guard
         proud
         silent
         no breath of wind blew
            where i slept

i dreamed i was a single moment
   in a single day
      in your single sentry's stance

momentarily you swam away to the horizon
   but returned
      gray
      obscene green
      luscious see-through blue
      brown
      purple — soon

your eastern horizon appeared speckled
   with little gray imperfections
   suddenly turned into white perfect sails

there you were
    in the now
        gone turquoise
        even gray
        returned coral blue
        sky blue

how are you so calm returning
    while so busy
        sombre-ness
            today
        sun
            another
        moonlight
            soon
        yellow reflections
            now
            from lime green mountain edges
            and dark olive brown ridges

behind me
    spotted stone walls of arabic origin

before me
    little blue boats
        with brush-stroked orange ledges
        and painted red bench seats
        washed white sides
        with ancient names etched in black ink

a lighthouse bobbing ahead
    whistling with rust
    singing a symphony of sounds
        adorned by color
    painting a picture
        with the noise of the sea

dusk is coming

daylight is leaving
    drawing definitive horizontal lines
        on vertical promises
        while i dream
            with a capital D

and you
    *chère la Grande Bleue*
        are like the helium balloon
        registering the rise of warm
            the fall of moist
            the air going hot and cold
            seldom any normalcy between

thank you
i am now seeking the sign that says
    this way to heaven
    and it points to Collioure!

# WAITING

*[written in Amsterdam]*


luscious tall girls
in narrow cubicles
glowing skin
ravenous brown faces
skimpy laces
waiting
    for the door to open

dark marble eyes
peering out of the glass
at some guy's ass
the look that lures him
into her universe
invites him
to drop a few florins in her purse
the look unduly wise
the look through the red light haze
the gaze that knows
waiting
    for the door to open

looking from the inside out
she knows what her world's about
through piercing eyes
expectant eyes
sad eyes
young old eyes
hands that know how to move
hands that know the groove
waiting
    for the door to open

wishing
    hoping
        wondering
            standing
                waiting
for the door to open

# JAZZ IN THE PARK

*[written in Bonn]*

big trees
soft summer breeze
    little children playing
    old branches swaying
water fountains gurgling
old pigeons chortling
    young woman being tough
    old man naturally rough
        around unshaven edges
red eyes
no surprise
    too much beer drinking
    mentality sinking
        to unheard of gutters
        with face smiles and mutters

flowers blooming
need little grooming
    sun shining brightly — today
    chill, ever so slightly — no dismay
people running
people working
    foreigners sunning
    foreigners lurking
      life the same — everywhere
solo travels
    as life unravels
      dreams unfold
        from stories untold
thousands of miles from home
alone
    not lonely
writing my tome
    for me only

*V.*

# for mom and dad

# TINA

*[for my mother, Katherine, departed January, 2002]*

every leaf
every twig
every flower petal
whether covered with dew in summer
    or ice in winter
was a thing of beauty for you

you and i walked together often
    when i was a young girl
hand in hand
    through the grasses in a morning meadow
        which jingled merrily when brushed by the foot
            'like a diamond pendant' you would say
            'gleaming and dancing' you would say

what you didn't know
    was that you had innocently paraphrased
        what thoreau said about similar visuals:
            'a literal wreck of jewels and a crash of gems'

you were a soul to admire
    a poet to listen to
        a gratified observer of all things natural
in the driving northern snows
    that lodged on your kitchen window panes
        you saw crystals
in a winter snowflake was a star
    and a summer dewdrop always contained a rainbow

you taught me
    about the eminence that attended pond waters at night
you taught me
    the luxury of musing in the sunshine of an autumn afternoon
you taught me
    that october was the month of painted leaves
    november was the beginning of early twilights
    and december danced with northern lights

then came january
    which you had not mentioned
when the angels called
    and you went willingly

goodnight sweet princess
rest in peaceful slumber
i couldn't have loved you more
i will not forget the simplest and most noble gifts from you
    your generous heart
    and your infectious smile

# REFLECTIONS

*[for my father, John, departed July 2007, with whom I travelled
to his birthplace in Molotschna Colony, Ukraine, 2004]*


### I. WHILE ON THE TRAIN

i try to understand
it was different then
there was a virginal faith
    an unlikely hope
        an unprecedented trust
things thrived here once
your mother sang and cooked borscht
your father planted fields that grew full and luxuriant
you and your siblings and cousins
    skipped about playfully
    swam in meandering streams
    squealed happily in and out of the school house

wars and revolutions blew everything sideways
it was 1924 for some
mothers fearful
fathers apprehensive
    grabbing their children
    grabbing some food and clothing
    heading quickly and quietly for train stations
    anxiously awaiting departures to foreign lands
        certainly not for vacation lands

a whole world
an entire life
    of innocent exuberance and consistent fulfillment
       renounced
       left behind
       abandoned
         in complete surrender
homes standing back in shock at their abrupt emptiness
    desolate and forlorn
    left in sudden stillness
    overlooking ghostly landscapes
empty wooden bowls left behind
    on makeshift wooden tables

it might as well have been a play
    ending its first act
    on a theatre stage
    actors temporarily out of sight
    behind the scenes
    to give room for a set change

whirring by on a new train this day
    eighty years later
visits to battlefields
    now cemeteries
visits to past villages
    now memorials
i try to realize the meaning
    of your disrupted history

i try to reconcile
    on your behalf
    the unnecessary infringement
    by evil-mongers and sedition
    by lawless intruders and excessive infliction
    by mal-intentioned insurgents and torture
        many moons broken
        and many suns shattered

i try to understand the reasons for such destruction
    chaotic havoc
    pernicious ruin
    egomaniacal disarray
    the reason: imperialist selfishness

i try to understand why things needed to be so broken
    for uncorrupted believers to be built up again
    the reason: supremacist selfishness

i try to understand the meaning of justification
    for so much meddlesome invasion
    for fraudulent slogans passing for solutions
    the reason: despotic selfishness

it is still the same landscape
    peaceful now
    with mirrored ponds
    wholesome gardens
    white egrets dunking for moss
    storks competing for nesting rights
        atop steep poles
        and granary roofs

how was it in your child's mind
    eighty long years ago
    all things half seen
       half heard
perhaps where darkness loomed in your father's mind
    you saw a big train machine
    come to a hissing stop
    and give you a happy ride
perhaps where sadness clouded your mother's heart
    you experienced miracles
    in your child's mind
    sleeping on cushions of cardboard
the adventure was indifferent to your pleasure
    and the destination pointless to your curiosity
was there excitement
did you see road signs
did you dream about a future
did you wonder

did you feel you were becoming someone

## II. A LONE MAN IN A SMALL FIELD

my father
   stepping across boulders of rotwood
      through tall field grass

bewildered glances
   up
      down
         left
               right
         forward
      backward
   all around

in search of a wooden abode
   that gave birth to him

no longer there

*VI.*

# heartfriends

# DAYDREAMING AT SEA

*[for Liliana Robinoff, written on board a Polish freighter
crossing the Atlantic to America]*


once
inside a tender pink sunset
we fused
into a passionate magenta moment
earth-soul
with cosmic-soul

now night has come
on the big sea
our moon
a venus moon
has wrapped its crescent around a single star
and is laughing sideways in the dark
i laugh back
and think
partway across the world
where your sky is filled with this same wonder
this same golden laughter

can we three
you
the sky
and i
join in our gladness
each in our own space
together
apart
distance being meaningless

i waved you good-bye
just then
just that
not forever

and then i slept
blissfully

## HEY GEORGE, WHY'D'YA HAFTA GO'N DIE?

*A Very Special Variation of Love*
*[for George Nelson, departed December 1984]*


how could you go and die on me like that
you were such a rare and precious friend
friends don't do that
friends don't die

you and i were the same age
we were the same age young
we were the same age silly

we were so in sync with one another
you and i
we felt the same about everything in life
    people
    relationships
    world events
    politics
    art
    theatre
    . . . and love

why'd'ya hafta go'n die

you were so many wonderful things
you were so many wonderful things to me
you were the epitome of purest friendship
you were the definitive of loving kindness and compassion
 among understanding human beings
  no matter the age
  the color
  the race
  the gender
  the sexual preference
  the social standing
  the education
  the belief

why'd ya hafta go

you were the first genuine and proud gay friend i had
and you made sure i knew that
you wanted me to know what it meant to be gay
what it meant to be born gay
what it meant to be born feeling something different
what it meant for you that wanting men was being born normal
you were always true to your feelings and your intentions
you did not betray yourself or others in any way
you were you
you were always openly you
you were born you
being born you . . .
    meant being a beautiful man who was gay
    and it meant being proud

why'd'ya hafta go'n die

in your life
i was a woman
i was your woman friend
but i was your heart friend
and you loved me as your heart friend

an affirming warmth always came from you
a warmth that revealed confidence
confidence about a real love of one kind
coming from and going to a human being
feeling real love of another kind

you always hugged me tightly with your tattoo-ed strong arms
you leaned your shaved shiny head against my shoulder
and you joked with me more than once about the 'jewelry' you
wore
and you said that if you weren't already in love with your alberto
you would have to be in love with me

oh why'd ya hafta go'n die

in early june of 1983
you left san francisco
you went to los angeles
you went to hollywood

you got there and hell broke open
you telephoned me to say you were sick and in hospital
you told me the truth as far as you knew the truth
you said you would get well

and you promised me when you got well
we would walk by the seaside
together
and splash around in the waves
and throw sand at one another
and play frisbee on the beach

somehow i knew you were in less good health
        than you were letting on

oh george, why you

you came back to san francisco for a visit
you said i should just take the afternoon off
what the hell . . .
we only walk certain paths once in life
you said

you and i were going somewhere
you said
to be together
to talk

you wanted to tell me you had effing AIDS

you didn't say it would be the last time we would see one an-
other
you also didn't let on how much pain you were in
all you wanted was to be together again
you said

all you wanted was to hear us laughing together again
you said

you didn't tell me you probably had less than six months to live

why you . . .

in august of 1983
a few days after our birthdays
you wrote me one of your poetic letters
you said
    dearest erika
    i so enjoy you
    your company
    your thoughts
    your spirit
    your joyful presence
    above all
        your understanding

    here i am
    at long last
    in hollywood
    unfortunately unhonored and unsung
    feeling capable at the moment only of doing my own weeping

    you are one of the few people in my life
    whom i can weep to
    you are one of the few people in my life
    whom i will always love

oh george
why did it hafta be you

and so you lived
a few more months

to the bittersweet end
    you lived
    you fought
    you cursed
    you got pissed off
    you fought some more

and in the end you smiled
YOU had won
not IT
not AIDS

oh, george

in mid–december of 1983 you took to the skies
your countenance radiating a translucent smile
i was told

but I knew

why did you have to go and die, george

someone found some papers in your room
someone anonymous
someone anonymous found your address book
and scattered notes
someone anonymous also found your last words to me

erika

i wish you a balanced life
as you continue your quest for clarity
in this unjustified madness

find an equilibrium that exists beyond daily survival
and too many obligations

please continue to bring joy into the lives of many

remain undaunted by challenge

laugh
talk
. . . or don't talk

most of all
be a living ambassador for me

love forever
george

oh you
my dearest friend
why did you have to go and die

you were a hero
you were one of the first soldiers
on that battlefield
that would turn into one of the worst wars ever

you walked a complex labyrinth
and it was threatening you with deepest anxieties

but you walked tall
like a proud warrior through the trenches
toward your permanent horizon

you gave yourself up with incredible nobility
you had no choice
you had no chance

you left such a void
such a devastation
such a senseless emptiness

why did you have to go and die

in the end
your spirit got trapped in an excruciating crisis
too soon there was no more room to move
too soon there was no more room to breathe
there was no more room to imagine
no more room for creativity
there . . . was . . . no . . . more . . . room

and so the light in you went out

and I cried
i mourned
i wandered aimlessly

a faceless
and heartless
and evil monster
had taken my best friend away

who would be my brother now

why did you have to die

with undeniable honor and grace and deepest pride
you lived
you loved
and then you succumbed
with others brave like you

you were stalwart
you were relentless
you were delicate in your angry moments
you were humorous in your outrage against this horrible disease
you were filled with perplexity
for what you intuited lay ahead
for unfortunate hundreds like yourself
who needed a good emissary

my dear george
you were a pillar
i understand your message now
AIDS crushed your love so unjustifiably

## CELEBRATIONS

*[for Melvin Manzano, departed 1989]*


knowing this calamitous june day
    was not ever to repeat itself
we dwelled a while longer
    on its accidental phenomenon
    a few castro blocks from home


reckless on a busy street corner
seen by the midnight sun frequenters
    in this friday night place
innocent we were
    though perhaps not to any eyes but our own


we live


do not ask whether life brings pleasure
    unhappiness
        blessings
            curses


we live


we breathe


the day is magnificent
the sky is marvelous
    with brilliant sunshine
    a reign of colors in the park
    and eucalyptus foliage
        rustling in the wind

we must celebrate

celebrate spirit
    it searches for us
    without restraint or shame

celebrate the body
    even though in the darkest hour
    it turns feeble
        weak
            blind

celebrate laughter
    smile at folly

celebrate tears
    cry about something we did

celebrate day
    the sounds
        conversations
            sights
                some days full
                    some empty

celebrate night
    the dreams
        mellow hours in retrospective contemplation
            even the sorrows
                and we've known many of those before

celebrate ourselves
     living
          sharing
               doing
                    breathing
                         dancing merrily
                              through paces of day
                                   and spaces of night

celebrate
     most of all
          the moment
               that gave us each other
                    and asked for nothing in return
          the moment
               that conceded to let us stumble
                    upon one another
                         and reap
                              such compassionate beauty

it was time to say thanks
     the following day
     for so much that had passed between us
     for the bright days made brighter

     — after a taste of thunder —

# EVENING TO MORNING

*[for Jack Cook, departed February 2011]*


obviously paradoxical
in your case
the direction became morning-to-evening

dearest friend
your exit from twilight was regal
peaceful
without complaint
exemplary

the early evening's rain-speckled lookout from my window
left me with suspended and damp sadness
remembering you
then a momentary appearance of the setting sun
painted a favorite frescoed dusk

in my tear-clouded mind
i heard a mandolin strumming
piccolo-ed velvet sounds of a life long ago
inspired by a paragon of unequaled kindness

this morning's mists feel heavy
a frosty chill hangs everywhere
but you
the antithesis of everything
would have noticed acacias across the street in redolent bloom

here in my warm space
i'm making my day
the way you would have ordered it to be
happy and always in the moment

with uplifted hands i will always dance for you
on this earth's ground
which you traversed completely
were so dedicated to
and have no become a part of

i dance for you
who showed my thirsty heart grace and passion
who always said to me: 'go, live, do it; you only pass this way once'
suddenly you have proven it all

it is my wish my eyes will forever gleam as yours always did
with leonine joy
with ferocious glow
and now pacified

# A QUIET GARDEN IN THE CITY

*[for Jerry Walker, departed June 2011]*

life dreams go on only so long
pills mainly corner the pain
and nothing is worse than sleeplessness
but we don't ask why
a quiet night is a blessing
even if it's dreamless sleep
what are those creatures
that hold you down
to force-feed the emptiness

ERIKA ATKINSON is author of three books, *Happily Lost in Time and Place*, *Frozen Stillness*, and *More Miles and Moments*. This is her first poetry collection, including pieces written over a period of thirty-plus years. She lives in San Francisco's Castro neighborhood.

95216315R00071

Made in the USA
Columbia, SC
08 May 2018